101 Tips for Parents

Richard Curtis

ISBN-13: 978-1499227994
ISBN-10: 149922799X

DEDICATION

To every parent, family and child I have ever worked with,
I dedicate this book to you, I hope my words helped.

Head on over to

101tipsforparents.com

for an exclusive thank you gift from

The Kid Calmer.

Richard Curtis

1. We learn the social graces of friendship through our parents teaching us not to snatch and telling us what to say.

2. If you walk to school agree with your child how far they can go ahead of you.

3. Teach your child young how to come down from emotional overload, help prepare them for the challenges of life.

4. Swimming clubs are a good way of teaching breathing techniques needed in anger management.

5. It is better for a child to leave a party five minutes early than fail.

6. We all experience chemical reactions like adrenaline, we need to teach children how to handle it safely. One way is by ending an activity and then extending it by a small amount to wean a child off the rush.

7. Meltdown tip – deal with consequences once things have calmed down.

8. Learning to ride a bike or a scooter help with core stability, something we use when we are writing.

9. You sleep better when you are relaxed and not stressed, so does your child. Make sure your family's bedtime routine helps relax them.

10. Behaviour is a symptom, good behaviour is a sign our needs are being met, poor behaviour is a sign they aren't.

11. Helping a child calm down is not rewarding their bad behaviour, it teaches them how to use their brain to self-regulate.

12. Have a password with your child for when someone else is picking them up.

13. Sometimes we need to cut the apron strings to let our children fly.

14. Be consistent with your consequences, a consequence coming out of the blue will often leave resentment.

15. Compromise is not the same as giving in.

16. Choose to ignore some behaviour, is it behaviour that distracts you? Is it constant little things? Is it behaviour that is done to push your buttons? These are things that can be ignored.

17. Rewards are important; we are rewarded for going to work by achievement or pay. We learn this during childhood.

18. If you have siblings sharing the same room, plan bedtimes to be at the same time or make the first one early enough that they are asleep before the second goes to bed.

19. Poo tip – if your child is holding poo, get them to blow up a balloon whilst sat on the toilet.

20. It can take up to six to eight weeks of consistency to change a behaviour and embed it.

40. Poo tip – try moving the potty into the bathroom to help the transition.

41. Teach your children the underwear rule, that it is not appropriate for people to touch them in the underwear region.

42. Are all behaviours worth picking up on? What is it teaching your child? Ignore some behaviours.

43. The way mathematics is taught is different to how we learnt, when doing homework ask your child how they like to do a sum.

44. Bargaining with a teenager is part of preparation for adult life.

45. Meltdown tip – come in from a different angle, talk about something unrelated or distract your child.

53. If your child struggles with friendships, have them play together in the lounge rather than their bedroom, so you can be on hand to guide them.

54. Putting things right may be enough of a consequence.

55. Do arguments always end the same way? Then change the words you use early on to change the outcome.

56. Dealing with a refusal? You could ignore it or ask your child what they would like to do after they've done whatever they are refusing to do.

57. Don't take away treat time, turn it on its head and reward them by giving them more. Give a child smaller chunks and empower them by extending the time as they succeed!

72. Food can be decorated with fruit or vegetables. A cake can have fruit on the icing.

73. Stutter tip – talk slowly and calmly to your child.

74. Games with concrete rules like dominoes, four in a row or card games teach us turn taking skills.

75. No matter how old your child is, do they still need you there when they have a friend round?

76. There is no stigma with asking for

    advice as a parent.

77. Poo top – if your child is holding poo,

    get them to blow bubbles whilst sitting

    on the toilet.

78. If your child runs away when you are

    walking with them, try stopping rather

    than chasing them.

85. Rather than having a battle about food a child doesn't like, but does eat, ask them what they would like with it.

86. If your child is anxious about missing you when they are at school leave something of yours with them.

87. Ultimatums rarely work, often the child oversteps the line to see if you will follow through and up the ante.

88. Eye contact is important in social interactions.

89. Share your positive emotions, they are infectious!

90. All behaviour has a meaning, good or bad.

91. "What did you do at school today?" is an overwhelming question, break it down or take it in turns to share news uninterrupted.

92. A large box can be hundreds of things, what can your child create?

93. If children will only settle in your bed, try lying with them on their bed until they are asleep.

94. Your child has done something serious, what do you do? Stop the whole family going to something, stay at home whilst the rest of family go? What is your family rule?

95. High levels of adrenaline over a period of time could cause a form of addiction, which causes side effects when coming off it or a chid to seek the rush again.

96. Stutter tip – devote time each day to let your child talk to you about something they want to talk about.

97. Good behaviour can be promoted through earning things, not by taking toys away.

98. Get your teenager to write their homework down in the lesson; then even if they don't remember, it's written down.

99. When was the last time you made a den with your child?

100. For a child who is anxious or concerned about their behaviour parties may be too much.

101. Share special time together by going
to the ball game together, don't be
frightened to share your interests and
let your child grow their own interests
and hobbies.

Richard Curtis

Tip index

Head on over to

101tipsforparents.com

for an exclusive thank you gift from

The Kid Calmer.

Richard Curtis

ABOUT THE AUTHOR

Richard Curtis, the Kid Calmer, has devoted his life to understanding and working with children and families and is renowned for his experience with children with special needs and severe behavioural difficulties. He has influenced the lives of thousands of children around the globe and has developed an excellent reputation for understanding what different behaviours mean. Richard runs thekidcalmer.com, a website to help parents with their parenting dilemmas and share strategies that he has developed. He also is the founder of The Root Of It, a team of professionals who help schools, families and children.

Richard lives in Southampton, England and in his spare time keeps chickens, grows vegetables and runs a children's theatre group. He is a teacher, has earned a Master's Degree based on working with children with behavioural difficulties and also holds several specialist qualifications.

Printed in Great Britain
by Amazon

THE BOOK OF FIVE RINGS

MIYAMOTO MUSASHI